YO-DNJ-910

Contents

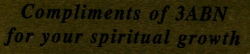

Compliments of 3ABN
for your spiritual growth

Three Angels Broadcasting Network
P.O. Box 220, West Frankfort, IL 62896
(618) 627-4651 • www.3abn.org

UNFINISHED BUSINESS WITH THE DEAD

**Mark Finley
and Steven Mosley**

Pacific Press® Publishing Association
Nampa, Idaho
Oshawa, Ontario, Canada
www.pacificpress.com

Cover design by Fred Knopper
Cover photos courtesy of It Is Written

Copyright © 2003 by
Pacific Press® Publishing Association
Printed in United States of America
All Rights Reserved

Additional copies of the book may be purchased at
http://www.adventistbookcenter.com

All Bible quotations not otherwise credited are from the
New King James Version, © 1979, 1980, 1982 by
Thomas Nelson, Inc. Used by permission.

ISBN: 0-8163-1989-8

03 04 05 06 07 • 5 4 3 2 1

A Gift in Grief

"It's been three months since Edwin passed away. I thought the pain wouldn't be so bad by now. There are times when I can't even move at all. There are times when I hear him at the door. But he's not there.

"I know I need to get on with my life. I know I need to get through this. Getting rid of Edwin's things are like getting rid of memories. And that's all I have— the memories.

"There was a time when this house was filled with music. I can't believe I actually complained that he practiced so much. My, how he could play! It wasn't just with his fingertips; it was with his heart. It filled this whole house with music. How quiet it seems now—and empty. Sometimes I think there's no more music left in this world."

People who have experienced a wrenching loss may know all about grief recovery; they may have all the answers in their minds. But it's their hearts that keep wondering: *Will there ever be a way out of this pain?*

Jacob had a rough and rowdy bunch of sons. They grew up in the hills of Canaan, about as tame as the foxes that preyed on their herds of sheep. Reuben was as turbulent as a roaring stream. Simeon and Levi were hotheads, prone to get violent whenever provoked. Judah chased wild women. Issachar's nickname was "rawboned donkey." This was a pioneer family, wresting a living from a sprawling wilderness. There was little room for refined manners.

But one of Jacob's sons grew up differently from the rest. No one could quite understand why. Maybe he got his sensitivity from his mother, Rebecca. At any rate, Joseph was a dreamer, a kid with his head in the clouds, even when he was tending sheep or threshing wheat.

And Jacob loved this dreamy son with a special love. He made a richly ornamented robe for Joseph, a coat of many colors. You probably know the rest of the story. The other brothers grew jealous; their jealousy turned to intense hatred. Finally they sold Joseph as a slave to some Ishmaelite traders who were passing through.

To cover up their crime, these brothers soaked Joseph's beautiful robe in goat's blood and told Jacob he'd been killed by a wild animal. It was a terrible blow to the old man; he tore his garments and put on sackcloth. Genesis 37:35 describes his grief. You can almost hear the sobs and the cries, the lament of the old man in the words: "And all his sons and all his daughters arose to comfort him; but he refused to be comforted, and he said, 'For I shall go down into the grave to my son in mourning.' "

One of the striking things about intense grief is that it *doesn't want* to be comforted. It resists every effort to diminish it. When you've experienced a terrible loss, you don't want hopeful words, you don't want to see the light, you just want to go down to the grave with your loved one. You know that he or she is irreplaceable.

Grief refuses to be comforted. Why? Because death and tragedy are so unfair. That's what the friends of a woman named Dorcas were feeling when she died. The apostle Peter came to visit them in their grief. And again, the Bible tells us that this grief, like Jacob's, was almost overwhelming: "All the widows stood by him [Peter] weeping, showing the tunics and garments which Dorcas had made while she was with them" (Acts 9:39).

What were those women doing? They were saying, "It's not fair. Look at all the wonderful things Dorcas did. She was always making clothes for the poor; she was always the first one to help anyone in need. Why did this good woman have to die? It's not fair."

Everyone who believes in a loving God has to wrestle with that question. When we're crushed by a terrible loss, our minds may understand some cosmic reasons, but our hearts can't let go of the face of the loved one. And we're left with an awful conclusion, the same conclusion that struck Mary and Martha after their beloved brother, Lazarus, died. When Jesus finally arrived on the scene, Martha greeted Him with these words: "Lord, if You had been here, my brother would not have died" (John 11:21).

If You had been here, Lord, my loved one wouldn't have died. Isn't that the thought that keeps running through our minds after a loss? The death of a loved one seems to prove that God has abandoned us. "He may be out there for other people, but He's not here for me."

Believe it or not, that's exactly how Jesus felt too. That's the question that Jesus expressed too. You'll recall that when He hung on the cross, the Savior was abandoned by His friends and disciples. He suffered alone. Most of the people nearby were His sworn enemies, cruelly mocking.

And in the midst of this wrenching loss of all human companionship, in the midst of Christ's unspeakable agony as He bore the sins of humanity, He lifted His head to the darkened, thundering heavens, and cried out in a raspy, breaking voice: "My God, My God, why have You forsaken Me?" (Mark 15:34).

Yes, God has experienced a terrible loss too. He knows all about the grief that refuses to be comforted. And His message to us is simply this: Yes, there's the pain of grief now in this darkness, but there will be a shout of joy in the morning. Morning does come!

Grief is a natural, healthful process. The shock, the denial, the anger—all the stages we go through—are ways the heart is healing itself. Grief for our heart is very much like a fever for our body. The fever itself is not what's threatening us. It's some virus or bacteria that's invaded the body that is causing the fever. The fever is the body heating up its defenses, making us rest so it can get on with the work of destroying those germs.

Fever is a symptom of the body trying to heal itself. Grief is a symptom of the heart trying to heal itself. Do you understand? Maybe a husband or wife has died; maybe a child whom you've longed for has been born dead—your first child. Possibly a teenager has been hit and killed by a drunken driver on the way home from school. Possibly you've been diagnosed with a malignancy, and your heart is breaking. You're filled with grief. It's not pretty; it's not pleasant; it's not smooth by any means. But there's a valuable work being done inside of you.

So in the weeks and months of intense grief following a loss, God simply tells us, "It's OK to cry, it's OK to feel angry." God even says, "I'll understand if you shut Me out for a while. I'll still be here in the morning. In fact, not only in the morning, but I'll be here in the midst of your grief and heartache and sorrow. I didn't forsake My Son, and I won't forsake you either."

Now we come to a question that many ask about grief recovery. What if the "fever" doesn't go away? What if the grief hardens into bitterness? What if sorrow sinks us into chronic depression? What if we keep repeating the cycles of grief over and over indefinitely?

Well, first we need to understand that different kinds of loss require very different periods of grief. The seriousness of the shock to our system requires varying times of recovery.

But still, grief is a process; it shouldn't be a permanent state. And so it helps to take a look at where we may come out at the other end. After we've gone through the initial stages of shock and denial and anger, we could use a bit of hope. So here are some ways that grief can finally turn into a gift.

Shirley always called the boy she and her husband adopted "our Christmas Boy." He had come to them during that season, and he had always led the family in Christmas celebrations. He'd start his Christmas gift list before Thanksgiving. He'd select and decorate the tree. And he managed to coax the rest of the family into singing carols.

The Christmas Boy had a beautiful voice. But just after he turned twenty-six, that cheery, bright voice was silenced. Shirley's son died in a car accident on an icy Denver street. He left behind a wife and infant daughter.

Overwhelmed by grief, Shirley and her husband sold their home—too many memories there—and moved to another state. They left their friends, their roots—even their church. And they could never bring themselves to celebrate Christmas again. No Christmas tree, no decorations. All that died with their son.

For seventeen years Shirley kept her grief as a barrier between herself and God. It was never quite resolved. She could never muster up the courage to visit her son's grave—even after moving back to Denver.

But then one wintry Christmas day, the Boy's daughter burst into their house, her arms full of packages and decorations. She was a young woman by now, full of her father's cheery vitality. And she informed Shirley that she'd be singing a solo at the church program and she wanted her grandparents there.

The next day Shirley and her husband sat rigidly in a church pew, fighting back tears. Then came their granddaughter's solo. In a clear, soprano voice she sang, "O Holy Night," and suddenly it seemed as if the Christmas Boy was there, making music again. It seemed possible to worship again.

Later, this young woman told her grandparents that she wanted to drive them to a special place. Before they knew it, they were standing at their son's grave. Shirley stood in silence, staring for some time.

And then, unexpectedly, her granddaughter started singing. "Joy to the World" rang clear and true toward the mountains. This young woman was carrying on the gift of the father she'd never known. She was speaking faith and hope, instead of bitterness. And as the last note died, Shirley felt a lump in her throat. For the first time since her son's death, a sense of peace came over her. Tears began to roll down her face, and she said, "I can live again." Finally she could say goodbye.

One of the things that can help us to finally resolve our grief is to realize that there are still ways to celebrate life; there are still gifts in the world. Profound grief makes us want to shut ourselves off from everything. We're numb. That's perfectly normal. But at some point we need to break open the door of our hearts. We can't let grief harden into a terminal kind of isolation.

The cherished voice of our loved one may have been cut off. But God's voice is speaking still. He's singing "Joy to the World," even though bringing us that joy cost the life of His beloved Son. He's been walking beside us through our darkest hours.

Listen to how David expressed God's faithfulness in that well-known Psalm 23. Down through the centuries, the twenty-third psalm has comforted thousands of men and women in their heartache and sorrow. David wrote: "Yea, though I walk through the valley of the shadow of death, I will fear no evil; for You are with me; Your rod and Your staff, they comfort me" (Ps. 23:4).

The rod and the staff were guidance symbols for the ancient shepherd. And David, the shepherd, realized what a wonderful Shepherd God had been in his own life. He'd been through plenty of dark valleys; there were many days during his time as a fugitive when he felt like giving up. But that rod and that staff were always there to give comfort.

God is with you. He's there with you in your deepest sorrows—even when you don't feel it. The Good Shepherd is always standing by. So find ways to celebrate life. You can begin in small ways. But please realize that it's still possible to worship; it's still possible to hear the music.

Human relationships are another way we can bring grief to a healthy resolution. We've got to find some way for love to keep going even though it may seem that love has died with our loved one. We need other people.

A story is told about a grieving woman who visited a holy man in China and asked him to help her get over her intense grief and sorrow. He told her to go get a mustard seed from a home that had never known loss or sadness. That would banish her grief.

Well, the woman went home to begin that process. And the next day she began visiting, home to home, in her city to make inquiries. But she could find no family that had not experienced some kind of tragedy. And the more people she talked to, the more she began to feel a kinship with them. Finally, this woman understood the holy man's point: Sorrow is banished when it is shared.

In the book of Job the Bible gives us one of the most beautiful pictures of comfort. Job's three friends hear about his loss of home and family and health. They set out to give what comfort they can. This is the same process of grief recovery that some modern psychologists record today. Listen to what's going on in the book of Job and notice how up-to-date and filled with penetrating insight this scene is: "And when they raised their eyes from afar, and did not recognize him, they lifted their voices and wept; and each one tore his robe and sprinkled dust on his head toward heaven. So they sat down with him on the ground seven days and seven nights, and no one spoke a word to him, for they saw that his grief was very great" (Job 2:12, 13).

These three friends didn't have any magic answers for Job right then. They couldn't explain the tragedy. But they could offer human companionship. They could be there with him in his sorrow.

Modern psychologists tell us that we do better in grief recovery if there are others near us. It's not the counsel they give; it's just the fact that they are there. Oh, how much we need to reach out to other people! Grief confined to yourself somehow multiplies. But grief shared becomes a much smaller burden.

When Frank Deford's eight-year-old daughter, Alexandra, died of cystic fibrosis, he knew that nothing would ever replace her in his life. During her long illness, Alexandra had shown such courage; Frank had learned a great deal about life from his little girl during the hours they cherished together. But now he wondered whether life was worth living without her.

Five months after Alexandra died, Frank's wife, Carol, dropped a suggestion. What if they adopted a baby girl? Frank didn't take to the idea, but said he'd think it over.

Actually, he thought it was a terrible idea. It seemed unfair to Alexandra. She was the one born to grow up in their house and be part of their family. It was bad enough that she had been sick and died. But to bring in some stranger to take her place? It seemed the final injustice.

But Carol kept dropping suggestions. Their son, Chris, thought the adoption would be a neat idea. Still Frank resisted. He couldn't find it in himself to let go of his perfect little girl. To him, she was a saint—an angel. There would never be anyone like her.

Then one day Frank and Carol were sitting on their patio, having a snack. Carol mentioned the fact that if they wanted a baby, they'd probably have to get one from another country.

"Yes, a lot come from South America," Frank said absentmindedly.

"Some very poor country," Carol added.

Then she reached over and took his hands and said, "Do you remember Alexandra's prayer—the part she made up herself and said every night?"

Frank looked at her. "Sure I do."

Then Carol repeated her daughter's words: "And God, please take care of our country, and bring some of the poor people to our country."

She stopped. There were tears in Frank's eyes. He finally understood.

Several months later Frank Deford visited Alexandra's grave. He held a baby girl from the Philippines in his arms, a girl he and his wife had named Scarlet Faith Deford. Frank told his newly adopted daughter, "You know, Scarlet, Alex really did get her prayer answered, and the answer turned out to be you."

And then he made a little speech to the wondering child. He promised that he'd never ask Scarlet to be Alex; he would never expect that. But he would tell her all about that brave, cheery little girl and hope that she would try to live the same way.

Frank Deford found a way to say goodbye. He found a gift, instead of just grief. He found a way to keep on loving, when it seemed that love was crushing him inside.

Each of us *can* find—somewhere, some way—a gift in our grief.

Jesus invites us to come to Him with our sorrows. He is the One who can mend your broken heart. Won't you give your grief to Him?

* * * * *

"Dear Father, we bring our broken hearts and our grieving souls to You right now. Sometimes the pain of our loss can seem so overwhelming. And it seems that You've turned your back on us. But please help us to see the Good Shepherd through our tears. Help us to recognize Your voice of comfort through our own cries. And please, by Your grace, enable us to turn grief into a gift that will enrich other lives. In Jesus' name, Amen."

Near Death or Near Life?

Sometimes it's hard to imagine that the cemetery is the place we're all headed. Such an uninspiring end to the wonder of life. It's lonely in a cemetery. It's hard to imagine that loved ones just turn into bones.

So, we've always been looking for a way out, a secret passage beyond death. And lately, we seem to have found an escape hatch, a window into another world. Perhaps there is an answer to the mystery of death in what people have been telling us about near-death experiences. Could that be possible?

Kimberly Sharp collapsed outside a motor vehicle bureau in Kansas one day. She lay there on the sidewalk, near death. People who stopped to try to help were shocked and terrified.

But Kimberly remembers those moments quite differently. She felt surrounded by a dense, warm fog. And in that fog she could see individual droplets of intense light and darkness. Then, suddenly, she had the sensation of an explosion underneath her, which spread out in a great living light to the farthest limits of her vision. The light seemed brighter than the sun, and Kimberly felt loved as she had never felt loved before.

Kimberly is just one of the thousands of people who are talking about their near-death experiences. Books about near-death experiences have become bestsellers. Tabloid television is scrambling to keep up with viewer interest on the subject with shows such as *Encounters, Sightings,* and *The Other Side.*

The number of Americans who believe that it's possible to have contact with the dead has jumped by 10 percent just since 1990. Pollsters report that some eight million individuals in the United States have had near-death experiences.

What are we to make of all this? Are we really getting a picture of the afterlife through these near-death experiences? Is this God's way of giving us a glimpse of heaven? Or is something very different going on?

One thing has happened that may help us better understand this phenomenon of near-death experiences. Now that a great deal has been written about near-death experiences, we can compare the different accounts. We can compare the various pictures people give us of what they saw during these experiences.

And when you begin to do this, one fact stands out: The more you hear about the afterlife from near-death experiences, the less clear the picture of the afterlife actually becomes. In fact, the picture becomes quite fuzzy.

There are a few similarities among near-death experiences, of course. People talk of floating out of their body, of passing through a tunnel, of being drawn toward a bright light. But when you try to get specific about what's really at the end of the tunnel, what's really in that light, the picture gets fuzzy.

Take, as an example, one of the most popular books on the subject—Betty Eadie's, *Embraced By the Light*. Betty says she saw Jesus Christ after her death. Lots of people have bought her book. They're interested in this encounter. But in the book, we never get a very clear picture of Jesus. He's a vaguely benevolent being of light. In fact, Betty can't tell where her "light" stops and His begins.

What's even fuzzier is the teaching Betty received from this being. It bears little resemblance to anything in the Bible. In her near-death experience, this woman supposedly learned that humans are not sinful creatures by nature and that there is no real tragedy in the world. It only seems that way.

Betty was informed that those who died in the Holocaust, for example, had chosen their fates before birth. This revelation was supposed to explain the problem of evil. But why would anyone choose the gas chamber in a Nazi concentration camp?

Betty also maintains that before she was born, she was a spirit being who helped in the creation of the world. These ideas may make interesting reading, but they hardly fit with Christ's New Testament teaching.

Here's another reason the picture from near-death experiences is fuzzy.

A man named Joe describes a strange journey he took while lying on his bed. It started with a tingling sensation in his toes. The tingling began to travel up his body, almost like a swarm of bugs, until it centered inside his head. Soon Joe felt as if he were falling through a gray, misty tunnel. Then, suddenly, he rocketed through the ceiling and found himself floating in a crackling, misty static. "It was like being in an empty TV channel," Joe recalled later.

Joe was so scared he couldn't even scream. But, finally, he snapped out of it and sat up in his bed, forehead sweaty, eyes wide open.

Now most people would say that this is a typical out-of-the-body, near-death experience. It's the picture of an individual heading out to the afterlife.

There's only one problem. Joe wasn't anywhere near death when he had this experience. He was just lying on his bed at home. He was in perfect health. He certainly wasn't on his way to heaven.

Do you see why the picture gets so fuzzy? Those who report they can travel outside of their bodies (they call it "astral travel") and those who report near-death experiences both report almost the same sensations. It all begins to sound suspiciously like it comes from the same source: our human imagination.

We can compare, for example, how people describe near-death experiences today, with near-death testimony from the Middle Ages. Yes, people did have these experiences in past centuries, and some recorded what they saw.

One typical story from medieval times involves an English farmer named Thurkill. He had a brush with death in 1206. What did he see? A terrifying corridor of fire and an icy salt lake. And this was just the early scenes! The landscape grew increasingly hellish as he went along.

Near-death visions in the Middle Ages had several features in common: a terrifying judgment scene, demons floating down, victims dragged through fiery rivers to hell.

According to a study done at Harvard University, the angry God and hellfire seen in near-death experiences from medieval times are interesting contrasts to the "nice guy in the sky" people seem to be meeting in near-death experiences today. Contemporary encounters with that ultimate being of light can be summed up in the phrase, "Don't worry; be happy."

Why this stark difference between near-death experiences then and now? It's safe to say that God has not undergone a personality change over the years. And we can say that the afterlife has also remained the same.

But what *has* changed? What has changed over the years is the popular conception of what God is like. Our mental picture of God has changed. And that's what we're seeing in near-death experiences. It's all bound up with what we imagine God and the afterlife to be.

Many people have a lot of fuzzy ideas about God and the afterlife. So, naturally, what they see in those near-death moments is pretty fuzzy, too.

I'd like to take you to one particular time and one particular place, where the picture isn't fuzzy at all. In fact, this is the first in a series of remarkable events that make the picture crystal clear.

The time? Around A.D. 27. The place? Nain, a small town in Galilee. One day, two processions collided just outside the gates of the town. The first procession, heading *into* town, was led by Jesus. Those who followed Him felt like celebrating. Some had been lame or paralyzed a few weeks before. But now they were jumping for joy. Others had been blind. But now they looked with pleasure on the wheat fields of Galilee. Some had been demon possessed. Some had been trapped in terrible sins. But they'd all been healed and forgiven.

Jesus was the One responsible for all this, of course. His procession was a lively and eloquent testimony to His power as the Messiah. It was evidence that backed up His claims.

Jesus' procession ran head-on into a very different procession, coming *out* of the town. Moaning and wailing erupted from this crowd. Everyone had a long face. People were tearing at their clothes and throwing dust in the air. It was a funeral procession.

A widow had lost her only son. It was tragic. Half the town was out to share in her great sorrow.

But something happened as these two processions meet head-on near the town gate. Jesus stopped the funeral. He stepped up to this grieving mother, and He said something that didn't make sense at all. "Don't cry," he told her.

Don't cry? This poor woman had every reason in the world to cry. And the citizens of Nain were quite busy amplifying her grief.

But then Jesus walked over to the open coffin and touched it. The bearers stood still. And Jesus spoke to the corpse, "Young man, I say to you, arise" (Luke 7:14). He said this as matter-of-factly as you or I might ask someone to get us a glass of water.

What did the corpse do? It sat up and began to speak! And Jesus led the young man over to meet his dumbfounded mother.

Now, what happened on that memorable afternoon outside the town of Nain? May I suggest that this was Jesus' picture of the afterlife? He was showing us a way out of the finality of death. And it didn't involve gray fog. It didn't involve a long tunnel. It didn't involve floating somewhere outside the body. It didn't involve human imagination or a vague brightness.

What do we see in Jesus' picture? We see a real, flesh-and-blood young man getting up from his coffin. He's all there. He's talking. He's walking over and embracing his mother.

What is Jesus' picture of what can happen after death? We can describe it with one simple word— *life*. That's the hope that Jesus holds out for His followers—life, eternal life. Not some kind of astral travel. Not just floating through space. Not just a ghostlike existence. But life!

What happens after death to those who believe in Jesus? Life. The promise is that we'll rise up out of the grave to a new life. We will talk. We will walk. We'll embrace our loved ones in broad daylight just like the young man of Nain. The picture is crystal clear in the Bible.

Jesus once described Himself in a parable as a Good Shepherd, and this is what He said about His plan for His followers: "I have come that they may have life, and that they may have it more abundantly" (John 10:10).

Life, abundant life. That's what Jesus offers to human beings who've always existed under the long shadow of death. He offers real, physical life—throughout eternity.The apostle Paul fills in more details of the picture. In his first letter to the Christians at Corinth he talks about how believers will be clothed in glorious heavenly bodies at Christ's second coming, when the dead will be raised immortal. Abundant life, not disembodied souls, that's God's promise.

Now, let's move to another scene that makes the picture even clearer. This event took place near the town of Bethany. Lazarus, one of Jesus' best friends, had just died, and Lazraus's sisters were inconsolable. They thought that Jesus should have come and healed their beloved brother. But Jesus didn't arrive until four days after the funeral.

When he came to Bethany, Jesus went directly to the tomb where they'd laid His young friend. He looked around at all the grieving people. And Jesus wept, too.

But then, He lifted up His eyes and uttered another one of His incredible commands. "Take away the stone," he ordered (John 11:39), motioning for some men nearby to roll away the stone, that large, round stone that covered the entrance to the cave, the tomb.

Martha, one of the sisters, objected. Her dear brother's body had been decomposing for four days.

There would be a terrible stench. What was the point?

But Jesus persisted. After a brief prayer, He called out, "Lazarus, come forth!" (verse 43). Again, it was a simple command. It was as if He expected corpses to obey His voice!

And do you know what? The mourners saw something move in the dark tomb. Lazarus came hobbling out, very slowly, still wrapped in his grave clothes like a mummy.

And Jesus commanded, "Loose him, and let him go" (verse 44).

Here, near the town of Bethany, we have another picture of the afterlife. It's broad daylight. No fog. No mist. No dancing lights. A real flesh-and-blood figure catches a deep breath as they unwind the cloths around his face. And he runs to embrace his incredulous sisters.

Real life, abundant life, because Jesus commanded it.

But there's something more to this picture, an interesting postscript. Lazarus actually became something of a celebrity. He had been buried—and he came back to life. Everyone wanted to touch him. Everyone wanted to talk to him.

According to some commentators, Lazarus was present during Christ's triumphal entry into Jerusalem. He may have led the donkey that Jesus rode into the city. He was Exhibit "A" in this Messiah's claim to conquer death.

But the interesting thing is that we have no record of Lazarus describing any kind of out-of-the-body experience during his four days in the tomb. If anyone could have floated out through what some call a dark tunnel toward that bright light, it should have been Lazarus. He had plenty of time. But the man was evidently silent on the subject.

According to Scripture, there's a good reason for this silence. The Bible tells us: "For the living know that they will die; but the dead know nothing" (Eccles. 9:5). And Psalm 115 declares that "the dead do not praise the Lord, nor any who go down into silence" (verse 17).

What is the picture we have here of death? Silence. No thoughts. No consciousness. And Jesus Himself paints the same picture. When He heard that Lazarus had died, this is what Jesus said, "Our friend Lazarus sleeps, but I go that I may wake him up" (John 11:11). Jesus consistently referred to death as a sleep. You don't do anything while you're sleeping. You're not conscious of what's going on around you while you're sleeping.

Please notice that Jesus and the writers of Scripture do not have a sentimental view of death. They don't try to explain it away. They accept the stark picture: Death reduces consciousness to zero.

This is something important to remember. If people are seeing things, if they're experiencing things, then they're not dead. If they feel they're moving out of their bodies, then they're not dead. They may be *near* death, but they're not dead. Because according to Scripture, the dead know nothing. That's the clear picture. There's simply no room for souls floating about in some state of limbo.

How then can the Bible writers speak with such confidence about eternal life? On what do they base their hope? How do we get to that other bright picture of the afterlife that Jesus painted? How do we get to real flesh-and-blood life after death?

Let's move to our final scene. This one will complete the picture for us.

It happened at a garden tomb just outside Jerusalem. It was early Sunday morning. Roman soldiers belonging to a specially commissioned guard shifted their feet in front of the large, round stone that sealed the tomb of the crucified Jesus. The first rays of dawn reflected off their spears and helmets.

Suddenly, the ground shook violently under their feet. The huge stone was rolled aside. And the tomb erupted in a blaze of light.

But what happened here was more than just the dazzle of light. It wasn't just gray mist and a dark tunnel. No, a very definite figure emerged from that brightness. It was the figure of Jesus Christ, very much alive from the dead. Matthew tells us, "His countenance was like lightning, and His clothing as white as snow. And the guards shook for fear of Him, and became like dead men" (Matt. 28:3, 4).

The Bible doesn't give us a fuzzy picture. This is an overwhelmingly real scene. The risen Christ was so real that the tough Roman soldiers collapsed in shock and fear. They almost had a near-death experience themselves!

But Jesus wasn't near death. He wasn't a mere spirit floating out of His body. He was quite alive, in a glorious, risen body. During the next few days, many eye witnesses would confirm this fact—people who talked with Jesus, and walked with Jesus, and touched Jesus, and ate with Jesus.

The picture of the afterlife in the Bible is crystal clear because it's the picture of Jesus. It's a definite face we see coming out of the brightness of the tomb. It's not just a vague sensation; it's not just a misty presence.

No, the eternal life the Bible talks about is centered in this Person, this face. Jesus walked out of the tomb. He broke through the chains of death. He leads the way for all who place their faith in Him.

That's what the collision of those two processions outside the town of Nain tells us. Jesus stopped the funeral. He stopped the weeping. He's the author of eternal life.

That's what the encounter between Jesus and His buried friend outside the town of Bethany tells us. Jesus spoke to the corpse. And the corpse obeyed His voice. Jesus is the Author of eternal life.

And, finally, Jesus' own resurrection shows us *how* it's going to happen. Remember what Paul said about believers rising from the dead at Christ's second coming? It's then that they'll receive new, glorious bodies.

Jesus' resurrection assures us that the dead will be awakened. Yes, death is a deep sleep. Yes, it appears that we lose everything at death. But there is One whose voice can penetrate through any tomb. There is One whose voice will call down from the heavens. And the dead in Christ will respond. They will rise—as surely as that young man at Nain rose from his coffin in broad daylight and rushed over to embrace his mother.

That's the wonderful hope Scripture offers us. That's the clear picture we find in God's Word. It's not just something we imagine when we're near death. It's far more than a long tunnel and a vague light. It's the face of Jesus waiting for us. It's His resurrection waiting to be repeated for all who believe in Him.

We can have confidence in that hope. We can face death securely in that hope. Why not make it your hope just now?

* * * * *

Dear Father, I'm so thankful for the hope that we have in Christ—the wonderful event of His resurrection that forever changed our future as human beings. We don't have to live under the shadow of death anymore. If we take Jesus Christ as our personal Lord and Savior, we can have confidence that His resurrection will be repeated for each of us at the Second Coming.

And so we place our lives in Your hands right now. We want to accept Your clear picture of the afterlife. We thank You for accepting us in the person of Jesus Christ. We thank You for giving us new birth into a living hope. In the name of Jesus, our Lord and Savior, Amen.

Unfinished Business
With the Dead

One of the hardest things about losing a loved one is this: the words that are left behind—words we can't change, words we can't make up for. Sometimes we wish so desperately that we could see our lost loved one again because of unfinished business weighing on our hearts.

And in our sorrow we wonder: *Is there any way of reaching out to them beyond the grave?*

A recent cover story in *USA Today* revealed some startling facts about the way people are coping with grief these days. Roughly, one in three Americans believes he or she has personally communicated with the dead. Apparently, this is a much more common phenomenon than we imagined. One in three believes that messages are getting through to the departed!

A new Gallup poll backs this up. Fully 28 percent of Americans say, "Yes, people can hear from or communicate mentally with the deceased." In 1990, only 10 percent of Americans would have agreed with that statement. Today, it's 28 percent. What's more, another 26 percent aren't sure we can communicate with the dead, but they aren't willing to rule it out altogether.

You may have thought seances and spiritualist mediums wouldn't quite make it into the twenty-first century. Well, they're hitting the big time.

The Sci-Fi channel features *Crossing Over* with John Edward. It started out as a late-night show featuring a psychic who claims to talk with the dead. But within a year, its audience boomed to more than 600,000 households and occupies a prime-time slot Sundays through Thursdays.

Edward's personal appearances are sold out weeks in advance. There's a two-year wait for a $300 personal consultation.

Both Nancy Reagan and Hillary Clinton are known to have consulted psychics.

Even the CIA has gotten into the act. That agency, along with several other U.S. Defense Department intelligence organizations, has spent twenty million dollars investigating paranormal communication. Twenty million tax-payer dollars spent trying to turn psychics into spy satellites!

The results? "Unpromising." That was the government's conclusion.

James Randi is a well-known magician with a skeptical streak. He has a standing offer of one million dollars to any psychic who can independently verify his or her supernatural abilities. The prize has gone unclaimed for four years.

But that hasn't stopped ordinary people from flooding to psychics and mediums for a way of getting through. And there's a very important reason why. As Randi puts it, "People not only want it to be true, they need it to be true. It's the 'feel good' syndrome."

Take Matilda, for example. She's an elderly Nebraska woman who lost her daughter, Cynthia, in 1974. Cynthia was a bright, lovely young woman who took her own life. Imagine the anguish this mother went through. Imagine all the unanswered questions. "Why, why? Is there something I could have done?"

After years of lonely days and nightmares, Matilda consulted a psychic. The psychic offered answers; she claimed to bring Matilda comforting messages from Cynthia's spirit. Cynthia was OK now. She was in a better place. She knew her mother loved her.

Who wouldn't want to receive news like that? Who wouldn't grab hold of that bit of comfort?

There's only one problem. And it's a serious one. The individuals that psychics claim to be talking with are asleep. They're not conscious. And you don't deliver a lot of messages when you're asleep.

How do we know this? Well, there's one Person who can speak with authority on the subject—Jesus Christ. He conquered death itself. He brought individuals back from the grave. He rose from the dead Himself—according to hundreds of eye-witnesses, according to people who walked and talked with Him after His resurrection.

Jesus is one Person who knows firsthand about "the other side." To see what Jesus has to say about it, let's return to the story of Lazarus.

When news reached Jesus that His beloved friend had died. He responded with these words: "Our friend

Lazarus sleeps" (John 11:11). And John, who recorded these words in his Gospel, says plainly, "Jesus spoke of his death" (verse 13).

You see, Jesus compared death to being asleep. He believed that conscious existence ceases at death. The apostle Paul taught the same thing. In his letter to the Thessalonians, Paul described believers who had died as those who "sleep in Jesus" (1 Thess. 4:14).

And there's only one thing that awakens individuals from this sleep of death—the second coming of Jesus Christ. Look at what Paul goes on to say, "But I do not want you to be ignorant, brethren, concerning those who have fallen asleep. . . . For the Lord Himself will descend from heaven with a shout. . . . And the dead in Christ will rise first. Then we who are alive and remain shall be caught up together with them in the clouds to meet the Lord in the air. And thus we shall always be with the Lord" (1 Thess. 4:13, 16, 17).

Those who have fallen asleep will awaken, will rise, when Jesus Christ comes to awaken them. That's the clear picture we get from the New Testament.

The dead are asleep right now. They're not conscious. So whom are all these psychics talking to? And how do they persuade grieving individuals that they're bringing back messages from lost loved ones?

Well, they do it primarily through something called "cold reading." What it boils down to is this: If you ask enough questions, eventually the client will lead you to the right answers.

For example, let's say a young woman wants very badly to communicate in some way with her dad. She visits a psychic. It's a long shot, she knows. But why not?

The psychic will ask her to think of some things she used to do with her father. And then, he'll run through some options: "I'm getting a feeling about the outdoors, something about hiking . . . no, camping out, or picnics."

At the word *picnics,* the young woman reacts—just a bit. Her eyes brighten. This provides the psychic with an answer. "Yes, you used to go on picnics with your dad. Those are wonderful memories."

The young woman is impressed. Yes, she *did* love going on picnics with her father.

Next, the psychic may turn to some object that the father gave his daughter. There are certain things most dads give their little girls. And he will usually fish for answers again, while appearing to be trying to track down an image from the beyond. "Yes, he's coming in clearer now. He's sitting on the sofa, and there's a little girl on his lap. I see something . . . a doll the child is holding . . . no, it's something soft and furry . . . a teddy bear, another animal, a pony, a monkey . . ."

Bingo. The young woman reacts to the word *monkey,* and the psychic knows he's found another bit of information to use.

With "cold reading," psychics can feel around until they hit the right answer. They rely on subtle cues that the client gives them to know when they've hit on something. And the grieving individual doesn't realize that she is the one who is really giving the answers.

James Randi has analyzed videotapes of TV psychic John Edward in action to see how he worked. Randi reported that the man had an accuracy of only 13 percent. In one interrogation of a TV guest, Randi counted twenty-three questions by Edward—which led to only three correct answers.

You see, psychics may be able to come up with comforting messages from the dead, but they're making them up. You could come up with something better yourself.

Well, if psychics aren't really the answer, is there any alternative? What can we do when we have unfinished business with lost loved ones?

May I suggest one simple thing? Talk with the living.

Talk with the living who have a real connection with the one you lost. Talk with the living. I believe that's what your departed loved one would want you to do.

First of all, talk with Jesus. Talk with Jesus about your sorrows, about your regrets, about your loved one, about your hopes and fears. Let me show you why that's a wonderful idea.

Here's what the Bible says about how Jesus identified with human beings: "Inasmuch then as the children have partaken of flesh and blood, He Himself likewise shared in the same, that through death He might destroy him who had the power of death . . . and release those who through fear of death were all their lifetime subject to bondage" (Heb. 2:14, 15).

We fear death for many reasons. But one big reason is that it cuts us off from loved ones, sometimes suddenly, prematurely. Well, Jesus came to free us from that paralyzing fear. He came to destroy the power that death holds over us, keeping us hostage to our hidden guilt, to our unspoken regret. Christ laid down His own life to free us from all these things.

And He does something more. Remember that phrase Paul used about believers being asleep *in* Jesus? In Colossians, the apostle presents that same principle in a different way. "For you died, and your life is hidden with Christ in God. When Christ who is our life appears, then you also will appear with Him in glory" (Col. 3:3, 4).

Our life is hidden away with Christ in God. That's true now. And that's true after death. He holds our life in His hands. He holds eternal life in His hands. And when He appears again gloriously at His second coming, the dead in Christ will appear gloriously as well.

That's why Paul says, "Comfort one another with these words" (1 Thess. 4:18). Jesus Christ holds our departed loved ones in His hands. The body may be gone, but He holds on to their identity. He holds their spirit.

So now, when we cry out in anguish, "My beloved father is gone. My precious child is gone," Jesus can answer, "I know, I've been there. I've tasted death for everyone. And I know how to keep safe that which is entrusted to my care."

When we cry out, "I have so many things I wish I could say," Jesus can answer, "I'm listening. I sympathize with human weakness. I can bring you comfort."

When we cry out, "I have so many regrets, so many things I can't make up for," Jesus can answer, "I understand your anguish. I tasted it at Calvary. But I transcended death. I am the Author of forgiveness and reconciliation. Trust your loved one with Me."

When we have unfinished business with the dead, we need to talk with the living. First of all, talk with the living Christ. He's the only One who completely understands both sides of the grave. He knows what it is to sorrow. He knows what it is to be cut off from His beloved Father. But He also knows what it is to break through the barrier of the grave. He can take us past our grief.

Second, we can also talk with loved ones who are living. That's another thing we can do. We can talk with those who remember that lost father, that mother, that child. Sometimes they can help us with our unfinished business in ways we hadn't expected.

When you have unfinished business with a loved one who has passed away, you want to communicate, you want to reach out to him or her. And it's tempting to chase after some magical way to get through, some shortcut beyond the grave.

But please remember this. Your unfinished business has nothing to do with those who make it their business to talk, supposedly, to the dead. It has nothing to do with paying a psychic to act as a go-between. Psychics are talking to themselves—or they may even be talking to something darker.

Unfinished business is about the living. The dead are asleep. They're not conscious. Your believing loved ones are safe in the care and keeping of Jesus Christ.

The One who understands all things has their destiny in His hands.

Unfinished business is about *your* needs, *your* emotions, *your* getting closure. And the best way to deal with those things is to talk with the living, talk with living loved ones. Talk with those who remember, those who sympathize. Get your regrets, your sorrow, out in the open. That's how you finish business with the departed. Talk about your good memories; celebrate the good times. Share how much you miss that individual. That's a healthy way to have closure.

Above all, seek the comfort that Christ and His apostles share with us. That's your ultimate source of hope. It's your ultimate source of reassurance. Remember the message of the New Testament for those who follow Christ.

There is something you can know when you lay a loved one to rest. There's something you can be sure of when you look on his or her face for what feels like the last time. You can know that the next conscious thought this person will have is of Christ coming through the clouds. That's the next thing he or she will know after closing the eyes in sleep.

There will be no struggles in the grave, no pain or sorrow, no journey through some shadow world between the living and the dead. For the dead, only an instant passes between their last breath and the glorious appearance of Christ in the heavens.

I'd like you to look at the great resurrection chapter in the Bible—1 Corinthians 15. This is where Paul goes into detail about how human beings at last find immortality. "Behold, I tell you a mystery: We shall not all sleep, but we shall all be changed—in a moment, in the twinkling of an eye, at the last trumpet. For the trumpet will sound, and the dead will be raised incorruptible, and we shall be changed" (1 Cor. 15:51, 52).

This is God's great unfinished business. He, too, has unfinished business with the dead—and with the living. He will complete it when that trumpet sounds, when Christ appears in the heavens. That's when the dead in Christ will rise. Broken bodies will be mended. Frail bodies will become strong. Individuals who have crumbled into dust will be re-created, their personal identities restored.

We will receive glorious new bodies, celestial bodies that are incorruptible. They won't wear out or break down. Our minds will be made new, our senses heightened, our abilities expanded.

That's what God promises to do for our lost loved ones. In Christ they have a wonderful future. In Christ we will have wonderful reunions. In Christ we can experience eternal life together.

That's the comfort the New Testament offers. It's more sure than any psychic's question-and-answer game. It's based on the fact of Jesus Christ's resurrection. It's more hopeful than any message a spiritualist medium can make up. It's based on the place that Jesus is preparing for us in heaven.

Are you struggling with grief today? Are you anguishing about unfinished business with a lost loved one? Please, let God finish it for you. Let Him make up for the missing apology. Let Him say the unspoken words. He will speak wonderful words on that great day when He welcomes us into eternity. And He can speak the right words of comfort to you today.

Please don't fall for any psychic shortcut. Talk to the living. Open up to the living. Place your hope fully on the One who conquered death once and for all.

* * * * *

Dear Father, we bring our sorrows to You, we bring our deepest regrets. You know how we feel; you know our weaknesses. You have taken on our humanity. You have tasted death for everyone. And so we entrust our loved ones into Your care and keeping. We trust You with their destiny as we let them sleep. We place our hope in You and in Jesus, our Redeemer and Re-creator and coming King. We thank You for the eternal life that You have promised. In the name of Jesus we pray, Amen.

Three Easter Witnesses

They were the three skeptics, three people in the depths of depression and despair. They were the most unlikely individuals to make up some story about a resurrection of their Lord. And yet they were about to have an encounter with the most glorious event in history. They were about to become eyewitnesses to the unbelievable.

In this chapter, we'll look at this unique event through their eyes.

Mary Magdalene and her two friends felt numb as they walked through the streets of Jerusalem to the outskirts of the city. It was very early on a Sunday morning. The sun was just lighting up the eastern sky. The two women stared down at the cobblestones as they clutched burial spices against their garments.

Their beloved friend Jesus had streaked this pavement with His blood just a short time before. He'd stumbled along toward the place of execution with a cross on His torn shoulders. Those horrible scenes were still vivid. The women couldn't get them out of their minds.

The death of Jesus had meant the end of everything for Mary. The end of forgiveness. The end of love. The end of hope. She didn't want to live in a world that could not tolerate a man like this Rabbi from Nazareth.

As Mary and her friends began to walk up the hill toward the place of burial, Mary suddenly stopped. She realized that in her confusion and gloom she hadn't thought of one important obstacle. She hadn't thought of the stone. The women asked one another, "Who will roll away the stone from the door of the tomb for us?" (Mark 16:3).

At that time, tombs were sealed with enormous round stones that were very difficult to move even for strong men. The women didn't have a chance of budging the stone sealing Jesus' tomb. How were they going to get inside to anoint the body of their Master? He'd been taken down from the cross, broken and limp, and laid in a vault carved out of rock. It hadn't been a proper burial. These women wanted to perform this one last act of devotion.

But the stone stood in their way. They looked at one another. Not knowing what else to do, they walked on toward the tomb. At least they could pay their respects at the site.

Meanwhile, back in the city, a man named Peter huddled in an upper room with the other disciples— the door securely locked and the lamps turned down low. The hopes of these men had also been crushed by Jesus' death. Their Master had allowed Himself to be crucified by religious bigots. Where was the kingdom of heaven that He'd spoken so glowingly about? Where was the new era of mercy and justice

He'd claimed was beginning? Nowhere, it seemed.

The worst of men had triumphed. The cruelest had had the last word. If the Almighty wouldn't protect this spotless Lamb of God, how could *they* hope to survive? The disciples were sure it was only a matter of time before their enemies would burst through the door and put them out of their misery.

Peter was uncharacteristically quiet this morning. He agonized more than anyone else. This disciple carried an additional burden. He couldn't forget the last look he'd seen on Jesus' face. It happened in the courtyard of the high priest, Caiaphas. It happened when Peter denied for the third time that he knew Jesus. He'd betrayed the Man who meant everything to him. And now it was too late to say how sorry he was. It was too late to take the words back.

About this same time one of the other disciples, Thomas, was wandering the streets of Jerusalem alone. Thomas was a sensitive, rather melancholy man. The horror of the crucifixion had affected him deeply. Weeks before, he'd made a resolution. He'd been ready to come with his Master to Jerusalem, the city full of Christ's enemies. Yes, to come here and die with his Master. He'd said so (see John 11:16).

But now that Jesus really had been killed, now that He'd been so humiliated in His death, Thomas just wanted to get away. It was too painful to think about. He didn't even want to be around the other disciples, his closest friends. If he looked in their eyes, he'd just remember even more vividly what they all had witnessed—the bloody cross, the spear driven into Jesus' side.

And so Thomas wandered alone with his cloak pulled over his head. Anonymous. Hopeless. Wrapped up in his dark thoughts.

Mary Magdalene. Simon Peter. Thomas. These three individuals were about to meet the One they were mourning. They were about to meet Him in a most unexpected way. They were about to become eyewitnesses to the most glorious single event in human history.

Some people today are inclined to dismiss their testimony. It's so fantastic it sounds like the stuff of legend. It sounds like a hallucination.

But listen carefully to their accounts. Scholars who have studied all the evidence surrounding the Resurrection find that it's very hard to discredit these witnesses. It's very hard to poke holes in their stories. There is strong evidence, in fact, that they could not possibly have made up the encounter that utterly changed their lives—and changed the world.

Mary Magdalene arrived at the tomb on that Sunday morning with her friends, carrying spices to anoint the body of Jesus. But she discovered something very surprising. The historian Luke tells us about it: "But they found the stone rolled away from the tomb. Then they went in and did not find the body of the Lord Jesus" (Luke 24:2, 3).

The huge stone had somehow been moved. But so had the body of their Master. Their first thoughts weren't hopeful ones. They assumed someone had stolen the body. And this made them even sadder. Their beloved Jesus hadn't had a proper burial, and now it seemed that He couldn't even rest in peace.

But they were in for more surprises. "And it happened, as they were greatly perplexed about this, that behold, two men stood by them in shining garments. Then, as they were afraid and bowed their faces to the earth, they said to them, 'Why do you seek the living among the dead? He is not here, but is risen!' " (Luke 24:4-6).

Here was wonderful news, indeed. Jesus had risen from the dead! But that news just didn't sink in right away. These women had just seen their Lord wrapped in linen—a pale, blue corpse. His body had disappeared, true enough. But a resurrection wasn't the first explanation that came to mind.

In fact, the account in Mark's Gospel tells us that "they went out quickly and fled from the tomb, for they trembled and were amazed. And they said nothing to anyone, for they were afraid" (Mark 16:8). That was their first reaction. They were bewildered, afraid. That's understandable. Resurrections don't happen everyday.

But after a bit, these women gathered their wits about them and decided they'd better go and tell the disciples what they'd seen and heard. So they went to that upper room, knocked on the door, and crept inside. The women had important news: The tomb was empty. But note how the disciples reacted. "Then they [the women] returned from the tomb and told all these things to the eleven and to all the rest. . . . And their words seemed to them like idle tales, and they did not believe them" (Luke 24:9, 11).

This doesn't sound like people about to make up stories, about to start legends. The disciples found the report of a risen Christ incredible. They just couldn't get their minds around it. The empty tomb wasn't enough to change their thinking. It wasn't enough in the beginning. They couldn't switch from despair to hope that easily.

But Peter decided that he'd better check it out at least. So he hurried out the door with John, and they began running toward the place of burial. John tells us what happened. "Then Simon Peter came . . . and went into the tomb; and he saw the linen cloths lying there, and the handkerchief that had been around His head" (John 20:6, 7).

The burial cloth was there. But there was no Jesus, no body. How did Peter react? "Bending over, he saw the strips of linen lying by themselves, and he went away, wondering to himself what had happened" (Luke 24:12, NIV).

Peter couldn't quite grasp it. What had happened? The empty tomb, staring him in the face, wasn't enough. It wasn't enough to erase his despair.

But God wasn't finished with His surprises. A bit later, Peter experienced something that *was* enough to change his despair to joy. "Then, the same day at evening, being the first day of the week, when the doors were shut where the disciples were assembled, for fear of the Jews, Jesus came and stood in the midst, and said to them, 'Peace be with you.' Now when He had said this, He showed them His hands and His side" (John 20:19, 20).

There He was, standing among them. Peter and his fellow disciples could look into that familiar face. But you know what? They still found it hard to grasp at first. Luke tells us that they thought they were seeing a ghost. It was just too incredible.

And so this is what Jesus did. "But while they still did not believe for joy, and marveled, He said to them, 'Have you any food here?' So they gave Him a piece of a broiled fish and some honeycomb. And He took it and ate in their presence" (Luke 24:41-43).

Well, this was no pale, broken body! This was no corpse! This was the living Christ, the living Christ having a little supper in their presence! The disciples *had* to believe; they had to accept the incredible fact that Jesus really had risen from the dead.

The empty tomb hadn't been enough to overcome their despair. But this latest surprise, this unexpected visit, erased all their doubts. Jesus had indeed appeared to them, alive and well!

But guess what? That still wasn't enough for one man. One disciple still couldn't bring himself to believe this story.

At some point, Thomas came back to that upper room from wandering the streets. He really had nowhere else to go. And the other disciples met him at the door with breathtaking news, "We have seen the Lord!" (John 20:25).

How did Thomas respond? "Unless I see in His hands the print of the nails, and put my finger into the print of the nails, and put my hand into His side, I will not believe" (John 20:25), he declared.

The testimony of the other disciples wasn't enough for Thomas. He was so deep into his despair that their words couldn't bring him out of it. Thomas had to see for himself. He had to touch for himself.

Well, remarkably enough, God wasn't finished with His surprises. John tells us that Jesus met Thomas where he was, still tortured by doubts. "And after eight days His disciples were again inside, and Thomas with them. Jesus came, the doors being shut, and stood in the midst, and said, 'Peace to you!' Then He said to Thomas, 'Reach your finger here, and look at My hands; and reach your hand here, and put it into My side. Do not be unbelieving, but believing' " (John 20:26, 27).

Thomas touched the wounds in Jesus' side and hands. Thomas saw for himself. And that was enough. Thomas *had* to believe. He had to add his testimony to that of the other disciples. "Thomas said to him, 'My Lord and my God!' " (verse 28, NIV).

Friends, this is the right response to the most glorious event in human history. This is the right response to the weight of evidence regarding Jesus' resurrection. "My Lord and my God."

There is hard evidence that the tomb was empty that Easter morning. But if that's not enough, there's more. There is clear testimony from eyewitnesses of Jesus' appearing alive and well after His death.

But if that's not enough, there's more. There is clear testimony from Christ's closest friends that they touched and saw and heard for themselves. Jesus did indeed rise from the dead. He wasn't a hallucination. He wasn't a ghost. He was there eating a piece of broiled fish in front of their eyes.

"My Lord and my God!" What else can we say when confronted with the fact of the Resurrection? What other response is appropriate?

I don't think God has held back in giving us evidence of the Resurrection. He hasn't been stingy in giving us proof that Jesus rose from the dead. He's been willing to answer our doubts. But many times we hold back in responding honestly to this earth-shaking event. Many times we are stingy with our faith, stingy with our hearts.

The Resurrection can seem like something that happened long ago and far away—a little unreal. It can seem like old news. It can seem like just another religious doctrine.

But the Resurrection is much more than that. It's the most glorious thing that ever happened on planet Earth. It demonstrates that Jesus can indeed be the Savior of the whole world. It demonstrates that He can be your Savior, that He can be your Savior today. It demonstrates that we can have the hope of eternal life. It demonstrates that the tyranny of sin and death can indeed be broken.

"My Lord and my God!" We need that kind of response, from the heart, to the fact of the Resurrection. We need that kind of affirmation. We need that kind of worship.

Let me tell you what happened to Mary Magdalene shortly after she looked into that empty tomb on Easter morning. It happened before the message those angels conveyed could really sink in. It happened before she could grasp the fact that her Lord had indeed risen.

Mary had stepped back from the entrance to the tomb and was looking around, probably looking for some sign of where the body of Jesus had been taken.

And she spotted a Man standing nearby among the olive trees and bushes.

This Man asked her, "Woman, why are you crying? Who it is it you are looking for?" (John 20:15, NIV).

Listen to her response: "She, supposing Him to be the gardener, said to Him, 'Sir, if You have carried Him away, tell me where You have laid Him, and I will take Him away' " (verse 15).

At the moment this was Mary's fondest hope—just to be able to pay her last respects, just to be able to anoint the body of Jesus, just to be able to express one last measure of devotion.

But then the "gardener" called out to her, "Mary" (verse 16). He said her name. And suddenly, that day of mourning, that day of sorrow, somersaulted into the first day of a new era, the first day of boundless hope and joy.

It was *Jesus* who was calling out her name! She knew it. He was standing there with that same wonderful look of love on His face.

Mary rushed toward Him and cried out "Rabboni!" (verse 16). That was what she always called Him— "Rabboni," or "Teacher."

And Mary fell at Jesus' feet, overcome with emotion. She didn't want to lose Him again. She didn't want to ever be apart from her Lord.

But Mary had work to do. She needed to go and tell the disciples the good news. So Jesus gently told her that soon He would be returning to His Father and her Father, to His God and her God.

How should we respond when the risen Christ appears, when the risen Christ calls us by name?

Friends, we'd better come to Him, rush to Him. We need to fall at His feet and worship. We need to stay near to the risen Christ.

"My Lord and my God." That's the message of Easter in a nutshell. That's the message that rings out from an empty tomb near Jerusalem. That's the message that rings out from Christ's appearances after His death. He appeared in the flesh to more than 500 individuals after His crucifixion and death. That's the message that rings out from doubting Thomas, the man who touched the wounds of the risen Christ.

Is it the message that's ringing out from your heart today? Is it the good news that gives you hope and assurance today?

I invite you to accept the fact of the Resurrection as the greatest fact in *your* life. It's about your future. It's about your Savior. I invite you to make the glory of Easter the truth for you. I invite you right now to accept the risen Christ into your heart as your Savior and Lord.

* * * * *

Dear Father, thank You for graciously providing us with rock-solid evidence of the Resurrection. Thank You for the witnesses who confirm that Jesus did indeed rise from the dead to serve as our Savior and Intercessor before You in heaven. We affirm what Thomas said about Jesus, "My Lord and my God!" We, too, make that confession of the truth. We accept Jesus as the One who forgives our past and gives us hope for the future. Thank You for giving us such a wonderful Savior. In His name we pray, Amen.

Terror for Terror?

The toll of terror has been growing dramatically. A new breed of fanatic has been unleashed on the world—one who combines an incredible disregard for innocent human life with the most militant kind of religion. We look into the eyes of these suicide bombers and see something dark, cold, and evil.

And all the bloodshed leaves us with a haunting question: How do we punish such crimes? Does the usual idea of justice even apply here? What sentence could possibly make up for these calculated atrocities?

Premeditated atrocities. Meticulously planned disasters. That is what has broken out on this planet. And it shows no signs of slowing down. A new kind of fear is gripping people everywhere.

We don't know where terror will strike next. We don't have a good place to hide anymore. And above all, we're shocked at the hatred that drives people to randomly take the lives of scores of men, women, and children. How do you protect yourself from fanatics who don't mind blowing up themselves in order to make symbolic strikes against their enemy?

Well, we're doing our best to fight back. We're doing our best to find terrorist masterminds and destroy their networks. We're trying hard to track down those who use our freedoms to plot attacks on freedom.

But the difficult question is: What kind of justice do these people deserve? To many of us, the usual kinds of punishment seem inadequate. A well-publicized trial would only give terrorists a showcase for their cause and possibly a prime target for more terror. So, some suggest military courts as an answer. But what about punishing these crimes? Is someone who was going to blow up himself anyway really threatened by a death sentence?

That's a tough one. There has been talk of some pretty extreme measures. Some have even written publicly about the use of torture—psychological and otherwise. What would we be willing to do to deter individuals from committing more atrocities? It's quite a disturbing question. Should someone who has slaughtered scores of innocent people be tortured to death? Should we respond with terror for terror? Few of us imagined just a few years ago that we would be asking that question.

I suggest we step back and get a wider perspective. I suggest we consider what God's options are as He deals with the wicked after the final judgment. This can help us clarify our attitudes. Think about it. God is going to have to punish some pretty terrible characters—Hitler, Caligula, Ivan the Terrible, to name just a few. What do these men deserve at the hands of God?

Well, here is where we get into a very touchy subject, because many Christians believe that the wicked are going to be tormented forever and ever in the fires of hell. It's something they believe they have to accept in order to remain faithful to what the Bible teaches.

At the same time, there are other Christians who say they could never serve a God who tortured people forever. This God doesn't seem to them any better than some blood-thirsty heathen god who demands human sacrifice.

It's a subject so touchy that you don't see very much written about it or hear it preached about today. It's something many of us would just rather not think about.

But I believe it's an important issue because it relates to our ideas about justice and retribution, and, above all, it shapes our picture of who God is.

Does God pay back terror for terror?

Can God demand eternal punishment and still be just?

Does a biblical faith require us to believe in eternal torment?

Now, maybe you made up your mind about these issues a long time ago. But I urge you to examine the evidence from the Bible. I ask that you look at the most important texts on this subject and keep an open mind. Because whatever our opinions about hell, we can always learn something important by going to God's Word. We can always get a better perspective.

Shall we do that? Let's study it out. Let's look at the evidence.

First, let's look at general statements from the Bible about what's going to happen to the wicked. What's the overall picture?

The apostle Peter gives us this straightforward statement: "But the heavens and the earth which now exist are kept in store by the same word, reserved for fire until the day of judgment and perdition of ungodly men" (2 Peter 3:7).

Peter predicts "perdition" for the ungodly. What does that mean? It means that they will perish, they will be destroyed.

The apostle Paul says the same thing. In his letter to the Philippians he writes about those who had become enemies of the cross of Christ. He says, "Their destiny is destruction" (Phil. 3:19, NIV). Jesus Himself made a similar comment. In His Sermon on the Mount He said, "Wide is the gate and broad is the way that leads to destruction" (Matt. 7:13).

"Well," you may be saying, "maybe 'destruction' really represents torment in hell, an endless kind of destruction."

But there's a problem with that idea. Bible scholars tell us that the Greek word translated "destruction" or "perdition" is the strongest word that could be used, meaning "utter loss of existence." You can't say it any more forcefully.

But let's look at a few more passages. Here's Jesus again, in one of the most famous statements He ever made: "For God so loved the world that He gave His only begotten Son, that whoever believes in Him should not perish but have everlasting life" (John 3:16). In this statement Jesus is contrasting two fates—everlasting life and perishing. Eternal life and death. The contrast isn't between living forever in heaven or living forever in hell. It's between everlasting life and perishing—death, destruction, perdition.

And now, let's look at a statement in Paul's classic presentation of the gospel, his letter to the Romans: "For the wages of sin is death, but the gift of God is eternal life in Christ Jesus our Lord" (Rom. 6:23). Again, we have a contrast between two fates, two possibilities—eternal life and death. Notice that Jesus and Paul did *not* contrast eternal life in heaven with eternal life in hell. They contrasted eternal life with death.

Some try to explain these statements this way: "Yes, sin results in death, the death of the body. Human bodies burn away. But the immortal soul does not. The soul can endure endless ages of torment in the fires of hell."

Let's take a look at something Jesus said. This may surprise you. Jesus warns, "Fear Him who is able to destroy both soul and body in hell" (Matt. 10:28). The passage is clear. It doesn't say "torment" soul and body in hell. It says "destroy" both soul and body in hell.

This is the first block of evidence we need to grasp. In the straightforward statements of Scripture there is one dominant picture of the destiny of the wicked. And that is—death. Apostles make the picture forceful. Prophets make the picture forceful. They all affirm that the wicked will die, perish, be burned up, utterly consumed, become ashes, become as if they had never existed.

So, why do people believe in a hell of eternal torment? Because there are other statements in the Bible that seem equally clear. They come from the book of Revelation. Here's a very sobering picture from Revelation: "And the devil . . . was cast into the lake of fire and brimstone where the beast and the false prophet are. And they will be tormented day and night forever and ever" (Rev. 20:10).

There you have it. "Tormented forever and ever." How do we get around that—those people who just can't imagine God torturing people eternally?

But there's more. In Revelation, chapter 14, we read about the fate of those who follow and worship the antichrist, that is, those who follow this beast and false prophet. Here's what it says: "And he shall be tormented with fire and brimstone. . . . And the smoke of their torment ascends forever and ever" (Rev. 14:10, 11).

Again, we have a pretty clear picture of eternal torment. And this leaves us with a bit of a dilemma. Because two views we're getting from the Bible on this topic seem headed in opposite directions. You have straightforward statements throughout the Bible that tell us the wicked will perish, be destroyed. And then you have these vivid pictures in Revelation of eternal torment. How can we reconcile them? It's like the irresistible force and the immovable object. Something's got to give.

Well, here's one important principle that all interpreters of the Word recognize. The Bible has passages that should be taken literally, and it has passages that should be taken symbolically. That is, sometimes a Bible writer is making straightforward statements; sometimes he is using symbols and metaphors.

The most obvious examples are the parables of Jesus. In these stories, a farmer harvesting his crop can represent God. Wheat can represent people. The book of Revelation is full of symbolic language. It belongs to a type of writing called "apocalyptic literature." It uses vivid images to represent events and forces in history. Revelation describes a lamb that opens a scroll, a dragon that wages war on a pregnant woman, and unearthly beasts that rise from the sea. No biblical scholar takes these images literally.

Now, when Revelation talks about a beast and a dragon, it's clearly using symbols. And so when it talks about their being thrown into a lake of fire, that is symbolic, too. And I believe that when it talks about the smoke of torment ascending forever and ever—that is also symbolic language. It's a poetic way of showing us the terrible finality of hell. The wicked will never ever have a chance at life or redemption again. Their judgment is irrevocable. It's forever.

In my mind, the most honest way to deal with the evidence about hell is this: Interpret the symbolic statements in light of the literal statements. That is, allow the literal statements to tell us what the symbolic images really mean. That lake of fire really is about death, destruction, perdition, becoming ashes.

It just doesn't make sense to do it the other way around, to use symbolic images to tell us what literal statements really mean. To allow the smoke of the lake of fire to tell us that death doesn't really mean death.

But here's the clincher. Here's something that makes it even clearer. There are actually literal statements in the Bible that point at those symbolic passages and tell us exactly what they mean.

Look at the prophet Isaiah. He's talking about God's judgment against wicked Edom. He says, "Its land shall become burning pitch. It shall not be quenched night or day; its smoke shall ascend forever" (Isa. 34:9, 10).

Now the land of Edom isn't still burning. The fire went out a long time ago. What, then, did God mean when He said "its smoke shall ascend *forever*"? He was using poetic language to emphasize the complete destruction, the utter destruction, involved in this judgment.

That's what the lake of fire is all about—complete and utter destruction. In fact, Revelation 21:8 tells us plainly that the lake that burns with fire and brimstone "is the second death."

The writer of the letter to Jude leaves us no doubt. Here's what he says about the fate of two wicked cities: "Sodom and Gomorrah . . . are set forth as an example, suffering the vengeance of eternal fire" (Jude 7).

Those cities are not still burning. But they suffered "eternal fire." What does that mean? It means permanent, eternal destruction. Gone forever.

The apostle Peter paints the same picture—in another literal passage. He tells us about the God who turned "the cities of Sodom and Gomorrah into ashes, condemned them to destruction, making them an example to those who afterward would live ungodly" (2 Peter 2:6).

The fate of Sodom and Gomorrah is an example of the fate of the ungodly at the end of time. Those evil people were consumed by the fire that fell from heaven. Here we have straightforward statements telling us what that smoke ascending forever and ever really means. Death really does mean death.

But there's still a bit more evidence we need to consider. There are, after all, very literal passages in the Bible that talk about a "weeping and gnashing of teeth" at the end of the age. Jesus Himself used the phrase "eternal punishment." How do we fit that into the picture?

Let's look at how this phrase, "weeping and gnashing of teeth," is used. Matthew 22 gives us one of Jesus' parables about the kingdom of heaven. It's pictured as a great wedding banquet. The guests assemble and celebrate the marriage of the king's son. But one man has come to the feast without a wedding garment. This was an act of great disrespect. So the king gives an order: "Cast him into outer darkness; there will be weeping and gnashing of teeth" (Matt. 22:13).

Why this anguish? Because the man realizes he's on the outside! He realizes what he's missing, that he's cut off from this marvelous banquet. Scripture always relates this "weeping and gnashing of teeth" to the pain of missing out, of being left outside in the dark.

Missing out on the wonder of eternal life—that's the great tragedy. That's the agony of hell. Yes, there will be "weeping and gnashing of teeth" in that final lake of fire. But it's not God arbitrarily torturing people forever. It's the indescribable horror of knowing that you're going to miss out on forever with God. You will never, ever, ever be able to share in the joys of life again.

That's why Jesus can talk about "eternal punishment." It's a death sentence that lasts forever. The *punishing* is not forever. But the *punishment* is. The writers of the Bible talk about "eternal redemption" and "eternal judgment" in the same sense. Christ's act of redemption took place at one specific time, but its results go on forever. The judgment takes place at one specific time, but its results go on forever. In the same way, the fires of hell don't go on forever, but its results certainly do.

But now, let's look at one last piece of evidence. Let's look at the "when" and "where" of hell. Because that will give us a final clue about what that lake of fire is really about.

Here's how hell happens. Revelation tells us that after the millennium Satan gathers an army together. And this is his plan: "They went up on the breadth of the earth and surrounded the camp of the saints and the beloved city" (Rev. 20:9). Satan intends to take the Holy City by force! He is still determined to overthrow God's kingdom and set up his own!

It's at this point that fire comes down from heaven and devours Satan and his followers. The next verse, verse 10, tells us that the devil is thrown into the lake of burning sulfur. Afterward, the wicked are cast into this lake, which is "the second death."

One of the clear implications from this passage is that the lake of fire exists right here on earth. Earth is where the final battle is waged; earth is where fire from heaven strikes and devours; earth is where the dead are raised to be judged. We have no hint in the Bible of any other place of destruction other than this earth.

But now, let's move on to the very next chapter of Revelation—chapter 21. The first verse tells us that God creates a new heaven and a new earth because the old earth has passed away. Verse two describes a New Jerusalem descending to the earth. And John tells us that he heard a loud voice saying, "Behold, the tabernacle of God is with men, and He will dwell with them, and they shall be His people" (verse 3).

Then we hear a wonderful promise: "And God will wipe away every tear from their eyes; there shall be no more death, nor sorrow, nor crying; and there shall be no more pain, for the former things have passed away" (verse 4).

This is what life will be like on the new earth. But remember, the previous chapter describes a lake of fire—on earth. Now, this presents an enormous problem—if we believe in a hell of eternal torment.

If people go on burning, how can there be no more sorrow? If people are still in torment, how can there be no more pain? If the flames go on and on forever, how can there be no more crying? If the wicked keep on suffering in hell, how can the "former things" ever, ever pass away?

Do you see the problem? We can't really have a new earth until evil and suffering are gone—forever! We can't possibly enjoy eternal bliss with God while millions writhe in agony in hell.

The good news is that hell does have an end. God does *not* believe in terror for terror. The fires of hell consume. That's what the Bible teaches—literally. That's the picture we're left with when we've looked at *all* the evidence in God's Word.

And it's a picture we can live with.

I want to look forward to a day when suffering is finally ended—for good. I want to look forward to a day when God really does wipe away every tear—forever. I want to look forward to a new earth where evil will never rise again. I want to look forward to a time when everything in all creation echoes the great truth that God is love.

That's my hope. That's my expectation. You can have that assurance as well.

Would you like to express faith today in a God of infinite mercy and justice, a God who will bring sin and suffering to an end? Can you believe in a God like that? That God is Jesus. That's the God of the

Bible. That's the One who offers you a way out of that final lake of fire. He offers you a place at His banquet table.

I invite you to accept His generous terms. I invite you to share in His wonderful grace. He deserves your trust. He's earned your allegiance. Believe in Him now.

* * * * *

Dear Father, thank You for sending Your Son to die on a cross so that we may not perish but have eternal life. Thank You for showing us the way out of sin and suffering. We believe in You. We trust in Your provision for us. We accept Your terms of salvation. We invite You to reign as Lord in our lives. And we make this commitment in the name of Jesus, Amen.

FREE
Bible
Reading
Guides

Call toll free
1-800-253-3000
or mail the
coupon below
Today!

$\mathcal{B}$ecome better
acquainted with your Bible

- *No cost now or in the future.*
- *Designed especially for busy people like you.*
- *Study at home.*
- *These guides will bring the Bible to life.*

☐ **Yes!** Please send me the
26 **FREE** Bible Reading Guides.

Name _____

Address _____

City _____

State/Province _____ Zip/Postal Code _____

*Please mail this
completed coupon to:* **DISCOVER**

 it is written • Box O • Thousand Oaks, CA 91360